sad birds still sing

FARAWAY

central
avenue
publishing

2019

Dedicated to my mother.

Published by Central Avenue Publishing, an imprint of Central Avenue Marketing Ltd.
www.centralavenuepublishing.com

SAD BIRDS STILL SING

Trade Paperback: 978-1-77168-183-4
Epub: 978-1-77168-184-1
Mobi: 978-1-77168-185-8

Published in Canada
Printed in United States of America

1. POETRY / General   2. POETRY / Love

10 9 8 7 6 5 4 3 2

sections

To whom it may concern:

If you are reading this,
you are still alive,
and since you are alive,
there is still hope.

sad bird sings

Society tells us
to break in silence,
as if the cries of our hearts
don't deserve to be heard.

Well,
I'll smile when I want to;
I'll break when I need to.

I will show this world
that it is still beautiful
when sad birds sing.

When I feel most alive,
I take a moment to take it all in,
to reflect on how low I've been
and how far away from it all
I am in that moment.

Those are the good days,
the highlights, the times
that have filled me with hope,
the ones that will bring me peace
when it is my turn to leave
this world behind.

How poetic,
the power of the heart,
to continue its beating
on the nights that we
wish it would stop.

Someday,
I will have
shed my skin
so many times,
it will be as if you
never even
touched me.

 — born again

I still slept on
the nights I thought
I'd never sleep again.

And every time,
I woke up with
the ground still
below my feet.

What more could
I have asked for than
another chance
to try again?

— train wrecks don't end the world

See,
my parents did
the best thing for me:
they showed me the
harshness of the real world,
but they never invalidated
my wildest dreams.

— raising dreamers

My most
valuable lessons
were not learned
in a classroom.

I walked this world
with violent footsteps
and learned through
earthquakes
and heartache.

I have shaken the world,
and it has shaken me.

Quiet moments,
when words are worlds away,
when not a sound is being made
but so very much is being said—
I live for those.

— eye contact

As a kid,
I'd chase the sun
and laugh as she'd run.

I've since grown up,
but I still play with the idea
that chasing sunsets
and chasing dreams
are kind of the
same thing.

It's less about holding
the sun in your hands,
and more about
enjoying
the chase.

— playing with ideas

There was no longer laughter;
this was how I knew it was over.

The loneliness I
felt with you taught me
to never underestimate
the power of simply
having someone
to talk to.

— how was your day?

Do not tell me
there is no light where
there is dark—that just
because we might break,
we should not fall.

I've lit matches in the dark,
and I have bones that are stronger
only because they've cracked.

— the healing process

On late nights,
I can't help but wonder,
wander barefoot
in my thoughts.

And I always arrive
at the same destination,
the very same thought:

"Better things
must await me."

There are worlds inside of me
that I have yet to discover.
There are lessons from my past
that I have yet to unearth.
I am still so young
with so much exploring
left to do.

— looking in is looking up

I write because
I have things to say
to people who
will not listen.

If happiness
can wander off,
it assuredly can
come back home.

— oh, and it will

All of this confusion
will make sense someday.
"Why?" will become an
answered question, and the
fog that clouds your mind
will leave your body
with the ease
of an exhale.

— breathing again

You can't force positivity
into a mind stuffed with negative
ways of thinking; some thoughts
have to go before there can be
room for something new.

— spilling your guts is really just making room

Sometimes,
all the goodness
in your heart is
all you have.

Oh, but how
incredibly far away
from nothing that is.

— infinity in your chest

I crave a
scene between us
so well written,
it bleeds through pages.

So much so
that at the end of the story,
after all is said and done,

all I can think about
is that one scene
and how it changed
everything.

Laughter: it can
alter the ambience
of even the
unhappiest
of moments.

— medicine for moments

If you find hope,
run toward it;
run toward this
unfamiliar light
and never
look back.

— first sign of light

I said it
the day we met;
years later, it is still
a pleasure to have
met you.

— "nice to meet you"

Because of you,
peace is a place I go;
it has lips, eyes, a soul
wrapped in skin, and
arms that restore me
whenever I have grown
too tired.

Find a lover who
makes the world feel
both bigger and smaller
all at once.

— hemispheres in my hands

You loved me as though
my heart were the world
and the world needed
more of it.

— p.s. it did

You
are a human,
not a rest stop;
do not let them
come back when
they are in need.

— self-respect

Do you feel it, too?

Tell me that I am
not all alone in this.

Because there is no
greater fear than being
all alone in something
that could last forever.

— and I am not alone

There were words
waiting for you in my pocket
no more than a moment ago.

I wrote them last night,
rehearsed them until
daylight broke and my
voice was cracking.

It's funny,
the way words
leave us
the moment we
need them the most.

— misplaced words

I used to believe
I was born on the wrong continent,
at the wrong time, in the wrong body
with imbalanced chemicals that
made me incapable of love.

— this was before you

We fell, together,
from the summits
of young love,
madly convinced
that falling
was the first step
to flying.

— young love

My only comfort
when I'm wide awake
is that we're still in love
when I'm in deep sleep.

If only we had met
later in life. Maybe then,
now, we would have been
mature enough for feelings
as deep and real
as ours were.

— young heartache

I still associate
your calm embrace
with some of the most
chaotic days of my life.

— the calm and the chaotic

Beauty is one thing,
but a pure heart, that
is beautiful.

Who's to say
you cannot start over?
Who's to say you weren't
meant for something else?
Tell me, when did it become
your place to tell me that I am
not meant for something better
than what I have now?

— I'll dream bigger if I so wish

I hope you realize
this someday soon:
true happiness isn't
sexually transmitted.

Never again
will I bow to my fears
so religiously; there's no
god to be found in
apprehension.

— forgetting fear

This heart of mine,
it doesn't break with every beat
like it used to; my heartbeat
is no longer a metronome
of misery. I take chances now,
knowing damn well that I
just might fall apart,
understanding that allowing
heartache to deter you from love
is no life at all.

My heart sings
a different song these days.
Can you hear that?
It is my soul swooning
over who I have become.

— the song my soul sings lately

A dream is a very real thing.
I'd know: I've felt it.
I've lived it. I taste
it on my lips every time
you kiss me goodnight.

— the taste of dreams

I owe my life
to close calls, the way
all of the knives in my back
have missed my heart
by centimeters.

— you missed

If the stars
are not aligned,
I've always found
it best to tug them
into place.

— why wait?

What an odd
statement to make,
but maybe, just maybe,
if I repeat it enough,
it will become
a part of me.

— "I am enough"

I can't explain
why I feel so much
when not a word
between us
is exchanged.

— silence, I swear, it moves mountains

If love can fade,
then so can pain.

The best
place to get lost
is in the eyes
of someone
you've missed.

— lost yet home

One hello
can take away
the pain of
a thousand
goodbyes.

Your lips
make me forgetful;
they meet mine, and I
can never quite remember
what I was so
upset about.

— suddenly amnesic

There is no
space between us,
even when there is
space between us.

Isn't that something
utterly remarkable?

It's as if this world could
never tear us apart.

— knotted at the soul

There's no hiding
from your soul mate:
they will find you,
you will fall,
and they
will stay.

Don't go thinking it wasn't real;
we don't dedicate ourselves
to things we don't believe in,
and at one point, we belonged
entirely unto each other.

— it was beautiful, and I regret nothing

You are not wrong
for wanting better
for yourself, but
you are wrong
if that means
destroying
someone else.

— there's enough sunlight for us all

If I die alone,
build my tomb for two,
just in case my soul mate
is born in a different
time than I.

— separated by centuries

I no longer long for
the worlds I've left behind.
I am no longer dinner for
the things that've been
eating me alive.

— maybe this is what closure feels like

the bad days

Loneliness—
it goes as unnoticed
as a heart murmur.

Until one day,
you begin to question,
"What is that sound?"

You hear it for a while;
it begins to be a bother.

Your heart skips
and you sink a bit
when you finally
understand it:

It's your heart crying out,
"I am alone, and I am lonely."

Lately,
my soul has been suffering.
I used to move mountains;
these days, I can hardly move
my own body weight.

I once believed in myself,
but times have never been harder.

This, right here,
is the part that hurts:
the fact that I let the world
seep into me
and drench my spirit
in negativity.

— I guess the world got to me

The universe shrinks
on the bad days,
when depression
is at its worst—
sometimes, down
to the size of just
this bedroom.

— the shrinking universe

Of all the
people I've hurt,
I've hurt myself
the most; I owe
myself
an apology.

It's as if
my lungs forget how to breathe,
my legs forget how to walk,
my heart forgets a few beats,
when my mind forgets
whose side it is on.

— Ativan adventures

Look at it this way:
you tried; you truly gave
something your everything,
and that's not something
to be disappointed about.

There are things holding onto you.
Kick them from off of your ankles,
those ghosts you're better without.

And when they squeeze tightly,
hold on for very dear life, you kick
and kick and kick until they let go.

They will give up—they always do.
You just have to keep pushing them
out of your life for long enough.

Your happiness today is far more
important than the happiness
you have had in the past.

We hurt together, always,
taking turns crying on the other's
shoulder, failing to realize that
the drowning can't save the drowning.
They can only pull each other a little bit
further under water.

— going down together

To forgive and forget,
how perfect would that be?

If I stopped believing in ghosts,
would the hauntings go away?

There are so many things
I am dying to unlive and unlearn,

but how could I possibly forget
what I still feel in my bones?

I swear,
some memories have a way

of forever feeling
like they happened today.

I'm feeling so little today.
It's not that I'm feeling small;
it's that I'm hardly feeling
anything at all.

— little human

Some nights,
I go out and drive
at twice the speed limit,
attempting to feel half as alive
as you used to make me feel.

— yet my heart hardly races

The worst part about
being an open book is the
people who turn your pages
and find nothing beautiful
worth sticking around for.

— in their eyes

I lost you, and the world mourned with me: the birds stopped singing, the flowers in the cracks of concrete all withered away, and the sunlight couldn't reach the ground through the cloud cover all summer long.

I am a world.

My heart is the most
problematic part of it.

It clashes with everyone,
threatens to drop bombs
if it does not get
what it desires.

And I know
far too well
that those threats
are the furthest thing
from empty.

It kills me to know that
you're out there searching
for somebody else when
I've been here all along.

— a friend who's dying to be your lover

Don't tell me it
was painful to leave
when you've never lived
through the winter that is
abandonment; this is
a cold your soul has
never endured.

— untouched

I keep this thing,
this picture of you,
the last one ever taken,
from the day
you died.

I take it with me
everywhere I go,
to remind myself
that if I can live on
after the greatest
loss of my life,

I can survive
today, too.

— I'm convinced you'd agree

Fight for me,
as I am fighting for you.
This love runs too deep
to be left up to fate.

— stars on our knuckles

It's selfish of me to think
I'm the only one in pain here.
Your lungs must hurt from all of
the screaming you've done.

My heart must have sunk
a hundred times by now.

A child shouldn't
take pills to fall asleep early, just
to avoid the summer storms that
rage nightly in the back bedroom.

My heart must have sunk
a thousand times by now.

Maybe if you understood more
about the chemicals in your head,
I wouldn't have to grow up feeling like
mine are the ones that are imbalanced.

I don't think my heart
could possibly sink
any further.

A deep sigh
isn't deep enough
to exhale the ache that
I feel inside of me
this morning.

— pardon my sadness

I'm getting better about it,
but it will always be there,
the dull ache of being
"happy for you."

Truly falling
asleep alone
isn't when there is
no one by your side;
it's when you feel like
you're not even
near yourself.

- I slept in an empty bed last night

That night,
the years I had
known you
disappeared, and
I no longer knew
the person that was
lying beside me.

You're a bridge that connects
who I am to who I used to be.

I cannot go near you anymore.

Because
I cannot touch you without
falling into ancient mindsets.

If I ever want to be a better person,
I must take this gasoline, pour it on
what I used to love the most, and let
the light cast a shadow in front of me
as I finally walk away.

   - a burning bridge and a lone shadow

Do you still fall apart
when you think of me, too?

— tell me you do

You say you've got
nothing left to live for,
as if I'm not standing
right here beside you.

— love is reason enough

I don't think you
fully understand
the gravity of
the situation.

If you stopped your
heart tonight,
mine would be
soon to follow.

— suicide kills

We don't ask each other
how we've been;
I'd lie to you,
and you'd lie to me.

We'd continue on
with painted smiles
until we'd run out of paint
and break down in the
arms of our mothers—

separately, of course.
It's always separately.

— two kids in love

This thing you created,
this life, this human,
you were supposed to
love it more than
you ever did.

So don't pretend
to feel destroyed when
the creation begins to act
like the creator
doesn't exist.

— raise your children, not your voice

Every morning,
I wake up next to the fact
that you fell asleep with
someone else
last night.

— right where you used to sleep

"I hope you find
someone you deserve."

How painful
kind words can be,
when spoken by
the wrong person.

— you used to be that someone

It's astounding,
how someone can go
from taking away your breath
to taking away your will
to breathe.

— at least I'm breathing

Peace has always felt
a lot like bottle art, something
I can see and appreciate
but never quite feel
for myself.

— through the glass

I was half your age
the first time you made me
feel half your worth.

I still carry that
scar on my body from
the first time you stopped
seeing me as a human and
more as a soft place to strike.

I didn't have it in me
to return fire back then,
but I promised myself that
I would hit you someday,
where it'd hurt the most:

in the spirit,
in the gut,
in everything you are.

I'd strike you back
by living my life
being happy,
in spite of the fact
that you happened.

In the end,
it's the love you
give each other on
the bad days that
matters the most.

The spin of the earth
makes my soul dizzy.
It didn't used to.

Falling asleep feels
more like running away.
It didn't used to.

Kissing your lips makes
me sick to my stomach.
It didn't used to.

Saying goodnight feels
more like saying goodbye.
Oh, it didn't used to.

- why does everything feel so different?

I have a bad habit
of searching for
beauty in beasts
and forever in
temporary
people.

I turned the page and began writing a chapter without you. I lost sight and blindly wrote the story I thought I should be writing, but there was always a lump in my throat, a knot in my stomach I couldn't untie. Life was not right, but I spent most of my days convincing myself that I was simply in a period of adjustment—as if I had just walked out of a dark room and stepped into the light of day. For weeks, this did nothing: I walked into walls; I stepped on my own feet; I smiled in public and convinced a few people I was happy inside while knowing I wasn't.

You were the void I could not fill, the rhythm my heart was dying to feel again. I left this dark space and returned to you, went where my soul told me to go. And when I came back, you forgave me for all of that, understanding that sometimes even soul mates make mistakes.

We looked
good on paper,
but all you are
to me now is
just poetry.

At least
we still look
good on paper.

— us, in poetry

autumn evenings

Most of us are not born
with chemical imbalances,
yet they feed us pills and
convince us otherwise.

And when life is leaving our eyes,
and we are too numb to feel the
pain we once suffered from,
they claim their drugs as magic.

Emotional numbness
is not a cure for unhappiness;
sedation is not peace
for those who panic.

We are a different type,
we who've lost our way:

our brains are not broken;
it is our souls that need
renovation.

— broken souls and broken systems

I've come to find that I
sleep less when I dream more,
that I think less when I feel more,
that the best part about being
trapped in your mind
is that you have a goal:
to get out of it.

— I'm in my head a lot; I need to get out more

I could really use the
sound of an ocean tonight,
a gentle reminder that
there are bigger things
out there than what
I am feeling right now.

— open water

To everything I've ever lost:
thank you for setting me free.

I enter a library at night
when I close my tired eyes.

The shelves are all full of either
words I never said or
things I wish I never knew.

I lie there, in the dark,
and instead of sleeping,
I read.

Because
by the light of the sun
is where I learn about others,

but this library,
this quiet place I go,
it is where I learn
to forgive myself.

I'm constantly worried
about the stars and how long
they'll stay aligned for me.
When they come out again
tomorrow evening, will
the universe still allow
this dream to be mine?

— I talked to the stars last night; they told me not to
worry

You were most
beautiful at sunset:
the red glow on your skin,
it was as if your heart was
all over your body.

You would smile then,
and I would know it was real.
There was always
something about it.

I miss that smile.
I miss your heart.

— I hope you felt that, too

If I'm honest,
it nearly destroyed me,
but I'm thankful that
I found something
that meant so much to me.
It offered me the chance
of a lifetime:

the opportunity
to fall in love with
living again.

— gentle reminder

We shared so
many wasted nights,
but the nights were
never really wasted.

And even
blackout drunkenness
couldn't keep me from
remembering our time
spent together.

I swear,
youth
and new love
go together like
whiskey and
cigarettes.

— night-light

Someday,
I'll prove you wrong;
I'll become everything
you said I couldn't be.

I live for that day,
the look in your eyes.

— this is a promise to you

Yeah,
maybe I loved
a little insane,
but at least I
had the courage
to lose myself in
something I
truly wanted.

— I am proud of the way I love

I visited your grave today.

It's odd: tragedy has a way of
stretching time for us who live on.

Maybe that's why these past
few months have felt like years.

I can't really explain exactly
how today has made me feel.

My mind isn't made up yet;

just like my heart, it is split
right down the middle.

Mixed emotions are such
tortuous little things.

— mixed emotions

Spare
your wrists;
scar my lips—
you deserve love
on a night like this.

— self-love v. self-harm

Believe me,
you are stronger
than the monsters
that will follow you
to sleep tonight.

— I promise

As a kid, I thought you had
superpowers;
I grew up and realized
you're just an amazing
human being.

— for our mothers

Kindness becomes
more apparent
in dark times,
kind of like
how our hearts
seem louder,
more alive,
in quiet places.

— acts of kindness as a source of light

This has to happen,
for reasons you and I
aren't aware of just yet.

And though our minds
will break, our hearts
will carry on.

This is the end of us,
my love, but it is not
the end of our stories.

Blank pages lie before us,
and we are the authors of
every tomorrow we touch.

— how beautiful is that?

I don't regret
a single moment
spent believing you
were right for me.

My soul has grown
strong from the weight
of holding up my own head
when nobody else cared
to do it for me.

I'm still learning
how to be easier on myself,
how to remember more often
that I am only human.

— be gentle with yourself

I wish you had
found yourself before
you found me.

I don't blame you for trying,
nor will I ever regret trying.

But when you find yourself,
please, come and find me.
I'll be waiting for you.

— whoever it is you turn out to be

Maybe
it was never
about forever for us;
perhaps it was more
about showing us
what love feels like
as we await the day
the one we are meant for
arrives.

— acceptance

I hope you read this:
It wasn't a fault of your own.

Their arms, their hands,
were simply too weak to carry
a love as heavy as the one
you had placed in them.

I need less time alone.
It's too draining, having
4am thoughts all day long.

You see, sometimes,
casual conversation is
what keeps us sane.

— talk to me about the weather

Last night,
I had an epiphany of the heart,
a sudden realization that
everything will be okay.

— and so it will be

You somehow
always had a way
of making me feel
okay with myself.

I'm learning now
how to do that
on my own.

I'm chasing after
that feeling again,
the very same one
you introduced
me to.

— a thank-you letter

We lay there in the grass,
and I remember thinking,

"If this is all we've
got going for us,
this ain't half bad."

All we ever had
was each other,
but that was all
we ever needed.

When you look back on us,
I hope you don't only see
the parts that hurt.

It is so strange:
remembering
how you felt
is still enough
to make me
feel held.

— how could I ever forget?

I find peace
in the idea that
if you were made
for somebody else,
then I must've
been, too.

— our soul mates are elsewhere

The cost of
forgetting it all
is far too high.
To lose the pain,
I would be forced to lose
years worth of happiness,
and I am not
okay with that.

I don't want
to forget;
I want to be
okay with
remembering.

To the friends I have abandoned:

I am so sorry
for cutting you off.

Anxiety has found a home
deep within my bones.

I shake in marrow earthquakes;
tremors send fissures through my soul.

A love for you still exists;
I feel it when I am most alone.

This island I've become,
it is not a permanent home.

It's just hard to be
around other people

when I can hardly stand
being in my own skin.

I lost my mind,
waiting on you
to make up yours.

How dare you love me
beneath one midnight moon,
only to make me miss you
beneath a thousand more.

— once in a lifetime

To be able to
look at you and feel
absolutely nothing,
that's the kind of
closure I want.

Take my heart. Add up the pieces—count them closely and carefully. Let me know if you love what you see. Is it too much? Do your feet drag from the weight? Is it not enough to keep you grounded here? Could you float off to somewhere else? I've always wondered how my gravity feels to someone other than me.

You can say
hope is dangerous,
but you can't say
it isn't beautiful.

Spew venom.
Break my heart if you
deem it necessary to feel
better about yourself.

But don't you ever
begin to believe
that you will be
the end of me.

Because
if there is more to life
than what we lose, then
there is more to me
than you.

I am not in love with you.
This is backseat boredom.
Hands are on my body,
but my nerves are all
somewhere else with
someone else.

— to pass some time

There are still
love stories left
to live, love letters
left to write.

Don't give up
on your heart
tonight.

unfinished business

All we have is now.
There is no time for space.

Let us bathe in mistakes
and dry our skin with
the fabric of forgiveness.

Come closer.
Let our atoms mix
and mingle with
one another.

We are far too young,
here and gone far too quickly,
to live as if we are afraid
to let somebody in.

In my
darkest hour,
hope kissed my
cheek and said,
"Everything
will be okay."

Some nights,
the bravest thing
that you can do
is continue
to exist.

Dearest Soul Mate:

You've been
so quiet since birth,
but my heart has been
fluttering lately;
you must be nearby.

I can no longer allow
the clouds of yesterday
to cast shadows on
the beauty of today,
to let unkind humans
leave scars that outlast
their stay in my life.

Be cautious with your company:
live with demons long enough,
and you start to become one.

— to burn in the sun

This story
is getting old;
I want to skip
a few chapters,
to a page on which
I am happy
again.

— old thoughts

I still believe
there is a right time
for everything,
even us.

The greatest thing
I've ever done is start over,
rebuild myself from the
wreckage of my own
brokenness.

— to begin again

Tonight,
don't worry
about how we'll
make it work—
just shut up,
feel my love,
and stay.

Anger—
it swallows you like
the sea swallows
a sinking ship.

And the most bitter humans
are those whose souls rest at
the bottom of this ocean.

They have drowned,
but you must stay afloat.

You mustn't allow this world
the privilege of drowning
the good in you.

        — it is far too necessary

Happiness
is when going to sleep
is no longer a means
of escape.

Some discoveries
make us feel just
a little less lost.

— search for those

It's more than just a need for
touch when it is cold outside;
it's a need to feel you, to be felt by you,
to be understood by you, to stay up
late at night poking holes in our souls
to expose secrets the world is far from
familiar with.

It's about opening up without the
breaking of skin. It's about stitching up
the damage history has caused us,
without sewing kits. Heartache has
pointed edges, but it's about forgetting
the fear of sharp edges and connecting
the fabric of our souls together,

entwining our cold fingers until we feel it
in our spirits, squeezing until we lose
blood circulation in our hands and then
squeezing some more.

It's about not feeling the pains and anxieties
we've been carrying around, anymore.
It's about breaking the walls that safeguard
our castle hearts without feeling broken or
broken into: I let you in, and you let me in.

Yet it's also about learning the decency to
politely knock before stepping foot into each
other's kingdom, because others have broken
down the doors and set our insides on fire.

See, I've been buried alive since I was barely alive,
but I am very alive now.

All it took was a knock at the door.

The most
beautiful part is,
I wasn't even looking
when I found you.

— blindsided by forever

I've fallen
in love with
your smile,
the way it
screams out,
"I survived."

It was all
theory before you.
But in late nights and
deep conversations, you
proved real what
was once just another
thought in my head.

— learning love

There is
a bright side
to everything.
I promise, if
you are suffering,
you just haven't
found it yet.

— the search must continue

A life well lived
is when the days
add up to more
than a lifetime.

When my mind
goes south, I chase
the North Star,
and it always
leads me
straight
to you.

It's a crazy thought, but maybe, someday, we're meant to come back to each other.

Through it all, you were the guardian angel I knew nothing about, the secret reason this universe kept me alive when I wanted my heart to stop beating.

Maybe
we just found forever
at the wrong time,
and someday, time
will pull us back
together again.

I still have
so many feelings
that have yet to find
a home in language.

— so much left to say

Just as my
ancestors before me,
I live my life shadowed by
the love of my mother.

I can feel it as
it follows me everywhere.

It guides me.
It embraces me
when I feel nothing.

It is, she is,
a part of me.

I am the continuation
of my mother, just as she
is the continuation
of hers.

We are all
the stretching of
our ancestors'
fingertips.

My lungs still burn,
from breathing in smoke
as I put out the forest fires
that once raged in you.

They are damaged,
and you are thankless in
the things you have taken.

And though I will
never await them,

I feel I am owed
a few apologies.

Get on top
of the world before
it gets on top
of you.

— before you're buried

Always carry some
extra happiness with you,
just in case you end up
somewhere awful.

— stuffed pockets

I've yet to know a pain
that couldn't eventually
be written out of me.

Because
letters are like strings
that are connected to our hearts.

The words, they tug at them,
making our hearts sing and dance,
releasing the feelings from our bodies.

Every flutter in your heart
is a melody this world
needs to hear.

— your song is so important

Whatever it is
I am meant for
in this life, each
passing day is
another step
toward it.

I am tiptoeing
        toward you.

Your facial features will fade as time goes on. I'll forget most
of the little details you know when you're close to a moment,
and I'll remember the darker, emptier
version of us: the bigger picture.

It was usually pleasant. It was sometimes unbearable. It was
calm most days. It was chaotic the rest.

Your hands were the loving, interlocked fingers that could
squeeze to break bones
at any given moment.

My words were both the cloud in the sky you'd rest your
body on at night and the dirt that would bury you when I
felt that you had made me angry enough.

The bigger picture, that is all I will
know someday: we were terribly good
for one another, until that was
no longer the truth.

Sometimes, it takes years, even decades, to truly understand why something didn't work out. Oh, but what a sweet revelation it'll be when I finally see where I've always been meant to end up.

Time was never
on our side,
but we'll love again
in a place where
clocks don't tick.

After you left Earth,
I was left in awe, wondering,
"How is the world still spinning
now that you are
no longer in it?"

In that moment, I realized
you're still here, living on
in everything your heart
has ever touched.

— and that is why the world still spins

You can lift me
from any darkness;
one hello, and I am
back in the light.

Not even now,
after all this time,
can I see myself
living this life
without you.

— love, again

For all the kids
growing up
mad at the world:
there's no point in being
angry at something
that feels nothing
toward you.

You'll find
the good ones,
the good humans.

Let them in.
Love them harder
than you ever
thought possible.

I promise you,
they are worth it.

In the end,
the universe had
greater plans for me.

I am living proof
that sad birds still sing,
that there is melody in
all of this madness.

Listen closely,
carried by the wind,
the world is breathing,
singing:

we are alive;
we are all still so very alive.

Do not go quiet.
Sing, sad birds, sing.

About

Faraway is an anonymous poet based out of California who, through his sincere words only, developed a massive online following in less than a year. He is also the author of *Homesick*.

@farawaypoetry

A letter:

I know, life has been hard on us,
but I can't name a time when things
didn't work out. Countless times,
life's claws have been around our necks,
but we are still here. We are survivors.

So when the world gets dark again, allow
your aura to overcome any darkness that
falls upon it. Smile in spite of everything.
Please, continue to care—you must.
This world is calloused, in dire need of
the touch of soft hands, ones that will
caress and nurse it back to health.

Be those hands. Be that softness.
Be gentle. Be everything this world
urges you not to be.

There is always a horizon to sail into;
there is always a song of serenity
to be sung. Sing it from your heart.

And as your vocal cords vibrate,
know this: you are changing the world,
one exhale at a time.

P.S. sad birds still sing.

With love,
    faraway